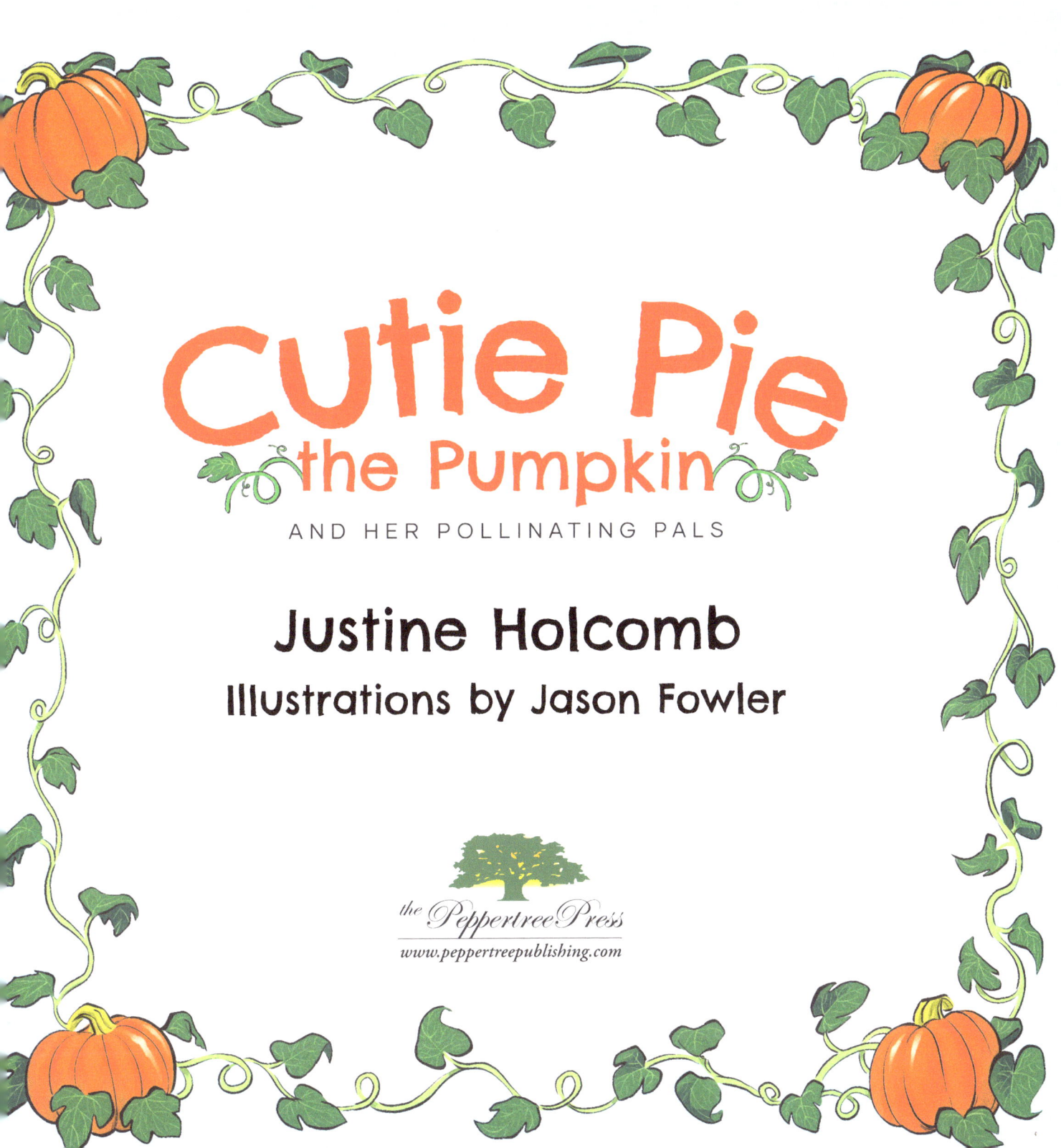

Cutie Pie the Pumpkin
AND HER POLLINATING PALS

Justine Holcomb
Illustrations by Jason Fowler

the PeppertreePress
www.peppertreepublishing.com

Copyright © Justine Holcomb 2023
All rights reserved. Published by the Peppertree Press, LLC.
The Peppertree Press and associated logos are trademarks of
the Peppertree Press, LLC.

No part of this publication may be reproduced, stored in a retrieval system, transmitted in any form or by any means, electronic, mechanical, photocopying, recording, or otherwise, without prior written permission of the publisher and author/illustrator.
Graphic design by Jason Fowler.
Illustrations by Jason Fowler.

For information regarding permission,
call 941-922-2662 or contact us at our website:
www.peppertreepublishing.com or write to:
the Peppertree Press, LLC.
Attention: Publisher
715 N. Washington Blvd., Suite B
Sarasota, Florida 34236

Hardcover ISBN: 978-1-61493-891-0
Library of Congress Control Number: 2023912584

Printed August 2023

For Luna, my amazing granddaughter, story time snuggler and pumpkin growing pal who makes my heart sing! I love you.
XOXOXO

With never-ending love to my children Alyssa and Griffyn. I'm so proud and honored to be your Mom.

To my Hubby, Oy!

Luna and her YaYa were on a mission to grow their own pumpkins for Halloween. With her light brown hair pushed back in her favorite polka dot headband and her freckles speckled across her nose like chocolate sprinkles on a cookie, Luna grabbed her gardening kit and scrambled out the back door with her YaYa.

"YaYa, is it really time to put the seeds in the ground?" questioned Luna.
"It sure is," chuckled YaYa.

Looking at the determined duo, it wasn't clear who was more excited about planting their fall pumpkins.

The twosome went out to the garden and prepared the soil by building four mounds a few feet apart for the pumpkins to grow in.

Then, with a poke of her tiny finger, Luna made four holes in each mound.

Next, she placed one pumpkin seed in each divot, covered it with dirt and said, "Ta Dah!"

Over the next few weeks, YaYa and her LunaBug (as her YaYa often called her) watered the pumpkin seeds, checked them daily and soon spotted sprouts on three of the mounds. Over time, they watched green vines grow and big orange flowers bloom. But there was a HUGE problem...

Luna STOMP, STOMPED her feet and plopped down on the garden wall.

"Why, YaYa? Why don't we have any pumpkins? It's almost Halloween!"
"It's a mystery of nature. For now, let's brainstorm new ideas to try next year."

Again, Luna (now several inches taller and another year older) went out to the family garden with her YaYa.

This time they only built two mounds instead of four. Next to the mounds was a new sprinkler system to help make sure the new pumpkin plants got enough water.

Just as before, long, bright green vines stretched across their brown garden. Just like their first try, giant orange flowers appeared. But again, they waited, and no pumpkins appeared.

STOMP, STOMP, Plop!

"Why, YaYa? Why don't we have pumpkins? It's almost Halloween!"
"It's a mystery of nature. For now, let's brainstorm new ideas to try next year."

Again, LunaBug, now more than half as tall as her YaYa and another year older, went out to the family garden. There were still two mounds and the sprinkler. Luna didn't see anything different. With a poke of her pink nailed finger, Luna gently placed one seed into each hole on the mounds. They watered and waited. Days went by and sprouts appeared. Then the bright green vines like neon lights grew across the soil.

"YaYa! YaYa, look we have orange flowers!" Luna announced.
"We sure do, let's check them out," YaYa responded.

The happy pair looked closely at each of the six flower blooms. They noticed a few more flowers along the vine that looked a little different than the others. The unopened flowers each had a small round bulb below its closed bloom.

"YaYa, do you see that round part on the bottom of the flower?" Luna inquired. "It looks like a very tiny baby pumpkin!"

"I see it," answered YaYa. "It sure looks like a tiny pumpkin. Let's go investigate why our flowers look differently. You may have just found a clue to solving our nature mystery!"

"YaYa, will we grow a pumpkin this time?" Luna asked.
"I hope so, we have tried and tried and never given up!" YaYa replied.

Once inside, the persistent partners used the computer to find out why their pumpkin flowers looked different. After reading and looking at pictures, they discovered the flowers with the bulbs were female flowers, and the other flowers were male. It was the female flower that could grow pumpkins—they just needed to be pollinated.

"YaYa, what does it mean to pollinate?" Luna asked without taking her eyes from the glowing pictures of pumpkins on the computer screen.
"Pollination is when pollen is moved from the male flower to the female flower so a seed or fruit can grow," YaYa explained.
"Ok, but how does the pollen move?" Luna asked.

"Great question!" YaYa put the computer down, slid her hand together with Luna's and said, "Come with me." They went to their garden and sat on the wall. Quietly, they watched the flowers and vines.

"What don't you see?" YaYa whispered.
Luna sat silently, thinking about what was missing. She slumped against her YaYa, stomped her sneakered foot and replied, "I don't know!"

"Do you see any flying bugs like bees or butterflies?" asked YaYa.
"Bees!" Luna jumped up and zoomed back into the pool cage like a firetruck on the way to a fire. "I don't like bees!" Luna exclaimed from the safety of the screened area.

"LunaBug come back," YaYa beckoned. "Bees are important pollinators and help move the pollen to flowers like our pumpkins to help them grow. Bees are pollinating pals!"

Luna reluctantly returned to her perch beside her YaYa. "But YaYa, since we don't have many bees or butterflies flying around our garden, how will the pollen move?" Luna asked.

"Well, since we don't seem to have pollinating pals to do the job, we are going to be the pollinators," proclaimed YaYa.

Luna stood up and stared at her YaYa. "I can't fly YaYa, I'm just a human, not a real bug!"

Hugging her close, YaYa chuckled and replied, "We don't need to fly to help pollinate. I'll show you how we can help our pumpkins grow."

The next morning, before the sun woke up, the pair crept out to their garden. A flower with the bulb on the bottom was open. It was time to learn how to hand pollinate! They took a male flower and rubbed a cotton swab over its middle. Luna whispered, "It looks like my fingers when I eat cheese puffs."

YaYa smiled, "Exactly, and what happens when you touch something with your cheesy fingers?"

"Oh, I leave sticky orange crumbs on everything," Luna giggled.

"Well, that's what we want to happen with the pollen. We want to sprinkle the pollen on the female flower, so it can grow a baby pumpkin." Gingerly they did just that. Then they crossed their fingers and made a silent wish for a pumpkin.

Each day they watched and waited for a sign that their pumpkin was growing. On the third day, they both screeched, hugged and did a happy dance. They finally did it! There, just below a wide leaf, lay a tiny green, round baby pumpkin!

Luna looked and asked, "When YaYa? When will our pumpkin be ready?"

One day, a few weeks before Halloween, YaYa called Luna to their garden. Luna sprinted out the door. YaYa was crouched next to their pumpkin with a huge smile on her face. "It's time!" YaYa exclaimed.

Luna stopped in her tracks, jumped up and down and clapped her hands in excitement.

Then YaYa very carefully cut the pumpkin from the vine. Luna leaned over and picked up their pumpkin and kissed it.

"Hi, Cutie Pie! We have waited a long time to meet you!"

With a slew of selfies, their precious pumpkin in Luna's arms, and a few more giggles, Luna peeked up at her YaYa. "We did it! We never stopped trying. Now our garden is not just a garden. It is our Pumpkin Patch, and we are pollinating pals."

At last, the tenacious trio went into the house so Luna could give Cutie Pie a long-awaited sticker makeover.

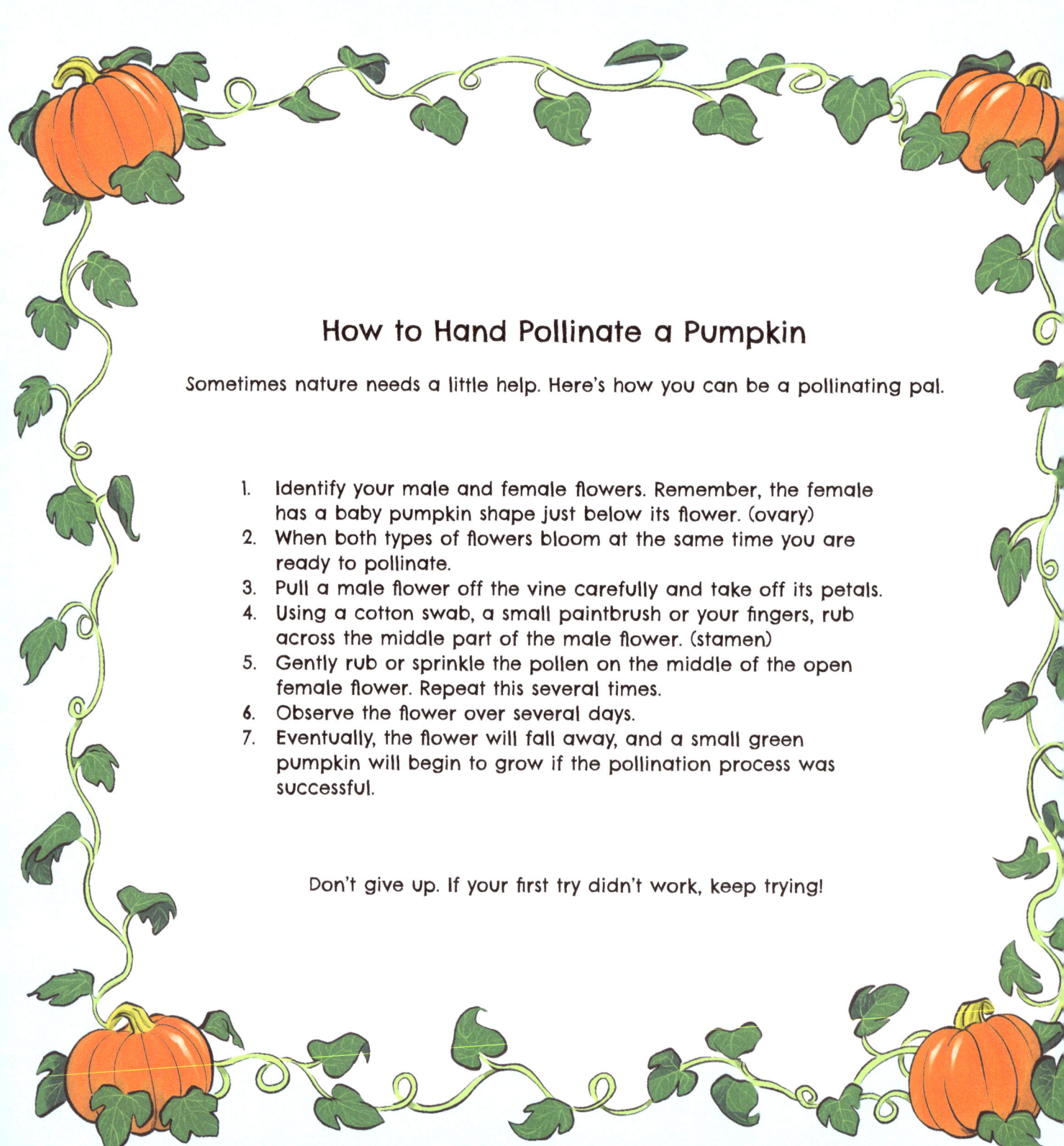

How to Hand Pollinate a Pumpkin

Sometimes nature needs a little help. Here's how you can be a pollinating pal.

1. Identify your male and female flowers. Remember, the female has a baby pumpkin shape just below its flower. (ovary)
2. When both types of flowers bloom at the same time you are ready to pollinate.
3. Pull a male flower off the vine carefully and take off its petals.
4. Using a cotton swab, a small paintbrush or your fingers, rub across the middle part of the male flower. (stamen)
5. Gently rub or sprinkle the pollen on the middle of the open female flower. Repeat this several times.
6. Observe the flower over several days.
7. Eventually, the flower will fall away, and a small green pumpkin will begin to grow if the pollination process was successful.

Don't give up. If your first try didn't work, keep trying!